THE 90 DAY PLAN TO MARKETING YOUR BOOK
WORKBOOK

MELISSA SE

CONTENTS

INTRODUCTION

In *The 90-Day Plan to Marketing Your Book*, you are able to stroll through the carefully devised tactics and techniques that lead to a bestselling book hitting the market.

When you have to market your own book, it can be a very powerful learning curve. Modern online marketers spend years gaining tertiary qualifications and building ironclad online strategies that they test over and over again by using a combination of strategic skill, statistical modeling, and keen research and documentation ability.

Once you have finished writing your book, you are expected to perform multiple roles: researcher, PR person, analyst, promoter, and strategist. The fast way to do this is to learn the basic skills required to make the kind of marketing decisions that result in better sales.

That is why I have created this handy workbook for you—the ideal accompaniment to the original guide. It will walk you through some highly important modeling techniques and research processes required to compile an effective book marketing strategy.

As you fill in these pages, you will see a clear picture forming. Your audience, purpose, and angle will reveal themselves as you gather and apply the research that you are going to uncover by using this workbook.

These fundamental research and marketing skills will help you take your book from zero to top selling in no time. With the right decisions, your book can sell thousands of copies, creating a revenue stream for you that will last for a long time.

Let's get to work!

KEYS

Time required for completion

Key goals

Observations

THE
EDUCATION
BLUEPRINT

"The goal of education is the advancement of knowledge and the dissemination of truth."
JOHN F. KENNEDY

This workbook is based on a sequential marketing process that will help you sell more books. It follows the same outline as the original guide so that they can be used concurrently for improved marketing results.

The first step is education. You need to know how to research your specific niche and what you should know about the specific storefronts that will help you sell your book.

How to Research Sales Knowledge

DAY
1-3

Run through this detailed checklist to ensure that you have covered most of the research basics when you are looking at the market for your book.

3 days

Market orientation, niche discovery

	Research Action Checklist	Check
1	Using Google, select 15 quality blogs on book marketing.	
2	Read their introductory posts on the subject in full.	
3	Narrow your research down to posts on your niche.	
4	Check major storefronts to see what is selling in your niche.	
5	Jot down the top 10 bestsellers' titles, covers, and blurbs.	
6	Locate the top 3 sellers, and see how these books were marketed.	
7	Look for social media, sales pages, and websites (build a picture).	
8	Jot down which formats are selling the most (epub, print).	
9	Think about what would make your book stand out.	
10	Record the latest niche sales figures from Amazon and similar.	
11	Find 5 blogs about first time indie book publishing & read them.	
12	Notice what angles are selling in your niche.	
13	Notice where opportunities are in your niche (what is not there?).	
14	Identify online infrastructure (for more, see web strategy later).	
15	Create 5 elements that would boost your sales based on this (elements can include covers, blurb, Facebook page, etc.).	

In the observation panel below, you are going to jot down any critical information you uncover during your research that could help you sell more books. Use it well.

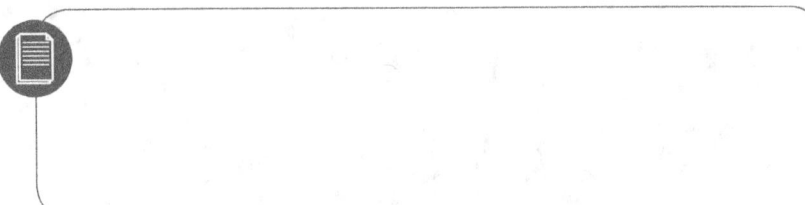

Evaluating Storefronts

DAY
4

There are many places online where you can sell your book. Today is about evaluating those storefronts so that you can orientate yourself in how they sell to the public. Compare each, and then make your decision based on this comparison chart.

1 day

Storefront orientation & selection

Storefront Sales Platforms		Fees	Top 3 in your niche	Top 3 overall	Visual appeal	Content	Requirements
1	Amazon						
2	Lulu						
3	Clickbank						
4	Payloadz						
5	eBay						
6	Barnes & Noble						
7	Smashwords						
8	Kobo						
9	Scribd						
10	Click2Sell						
11	PubIt						

This second section is to compare your infrastructure with the top five selling books on each core storefront platform. You will need a similar infrastructure in order to sell well.

Author Platform		Amazon	Lulu	Clickbank	Smashwords	Payloadz
1	Book Website					
2	Blog					
3	Sales Pages					
4	Facebook					
5	Twitter					
6	YouTube					
7	LinkedIn					
8	Wikipedia					
9	Pinterest					
10	Google+					

Based on the filled-in author platform sheet, what infrastructure does your book need for top sales? Arrange to have these created.

Platform Selection Criteria

DAY 5

The right book format will make sure that your readers have no excuse not to buy your book when the opportunity presents itself. You must decide which formats you will sell your book in based on the competitive research you have been doing.

1 day

By now there are at least 10 bestselling books in your specific niche that you have noticed on your chosen sales platforms. Detail which formats they offer, and decide based on this.

Format identification for optimum sales

Storefront Format Identification	EPub	iBook	Kindle	PDF	Mobi	Print	HTML
1	Amazon							
2	Lulu							
3	Clickbank							
4	Payloadz							
5	eBay							
6	Barnes & Noble							
7	Smashwords							
8	Kobo							
9	Scribd							
10	Click2Sell							
11	PubIt							

- Based on these details, which platforms are selling high volumes of your chosen format?
- Is there a platform where some formats sell better than others?

Figure out how much time and additional effort it will take to produce your book in at least four core file formats for your platforms.

Creating a Platform Strategy

DAY 6

A platform strategy outlines how you are going to sell on each chosen platform. To clarify this for yourself, begin by choosing four "best-in-class" examples from each platform to model off by conducting general research online. Then tier your platforms according to how much time you will dedicate to each, according to your chosen strategy.

3 days

Build marketing platform strategy & identify tiers for time/ resource allocation

Platform		Example 1	Example 2	Example 3	Example 4
1	Amazon				
2	Lulu				
3	Clickbank				
4	Smashwords				
5	Payloadz				
6	Book website				
7	Blog				
8	Sales page (microsites)				
9	Facebook				
10	Twitter				
11	YouTube				
12	LinkedIn				
13	Pinterest				
14	Wikipedia				
15	Google+				

Based on these discovered examples, rank where you believe the most book sales will come from. You must focus most of your time and resources on your top three platforms. I strongly suggest one of these platforms be your book's website for direct sales.

Rank/Tier by Order of Importance	Percentage of Time/Resource Allocation
1	40%
2	20%
3	10%
4	2.5%
5	2.5%
6	2.5%
7	2.5%
8	2.5%
9	2.5%
10	2.5%
11	2.5%
12	2.5%
13	2.5%
14	2.5%
15	2.5%

Remember, if it takes up too much time/effort/resources, it needs to be delegated to someone else and budgeted for accordingly.

Determining Your Financial Investment

DAY

7

Investing in the right areas will give you the best returns. You have already identified which platforms you will concentrate on the most. Now you need to determine how much it will cost you to market your book on your top three chosen platforms.

3 days

Determine what you should invest in each platform.

Platform	Setup costs	Ad costs	Ongoing content costs	Overall weekly budget
1 Book website				
2				
3				

Remember, 70% of your financial investment must be applied to your top three platforms. Everything else needs to work on a 30% split.

4				
5				
6				
7				
8				
9				
10				
11				
12				
13				

Assign a set amount to each platform that you can afford, and get quotes for the work you need done. Never spend more than you have projected. At least 80% of the money your book earns should be reinvested back into marketing for the first three months.

Goal Selection Blueprint

Your book marketing campaign needs an overall sales goal, and each platform in turn needs a sales goal. You need to create these using your platform strategy.

Example: To earn $7,000 in book sales on this platform over the course of three months

3 days

To set your main and secondary platform marketing goals

Book Website:

Main Goal	
1	
Secondary/Micro Goals	
2	
3	
4	

Platform #2:

Main Goal	
1	
Secondary/Micro Goals	
2	
3	
4	

Platform #3:

Main Goal	
1	
Secondary/Micro Goals	
2	
3	
4	

Based on your goals, how many sales do you have to make every day?

THE
BOOK PRODUCT
BLUEPRINT

"The aim of marketing is to know and understand the customer so well the product or service fits him and sells itself."
PETER DRUCKER

Your book is a product first and a work of art second. This section of your workbook is going to give you essential tools that you will need to build a product pack for your book. You cannot simply write a book and be done with it!

Images and other media matter in your sales materials. A super-powered marketing campaign makes good use of copy, images, video, and other content. Here is what you need to make sure that your book has what it needs to be a great product.

Designing Book Cover Materials

Your book cover is the one single sales tool that will sell your book on nearly every platform. That is why you need to know how to create one that works in your niche. Make sure that you follow these steps.

1 day

To create high-conversion book cover images

Your book cover pack should consist of:

Book Cover Pack		Check
1	6 x book cover images (in a range of sizes)	
2	3–5 high-quality author photos	

Checklist for Each Image:

	Image Checklist	Check
1	1 full A4-size, high-resolution book cover shot	
2	1 realistic book cover placed on a 3D book model	
3	1 realistic book cover with an e-reader 3D model	
4	1 readable book cover thumbnail, sized for the web	
5	1 readable book cover, larger size for the web	
6	1 book in your hands as an author	

Using The 90-Day Plan, create your one-liner here:

Add in your short paragraph here:

Building Influencer Lists

You need some top marketing content to help you sell, namely your endorsements, blurb, and testimonials. Using your guide, fill in these worksheet areas so that you can find influencers that will endorse your book.

1 day

Discover influencers that will endorse your book.

Endorsements (Names and email addresses of influencers):			
1		26	
2		27	
3		28	
4		29	
5		30	
6		31	
7		32	
8		33	
9		34	
10		35	
11		36	
12		37	
13		38	
14		39	
15		40	
16		41	
17		42	
18		43	
19		44	
20		45	
21		46	
22		47	
23		48	
24		49	
25		50	

Now create a standard email that you can send to all of these influencers asking them to endorse your book. In return, you can offer a post for their blog or another incentive.

Your Email Template

- Be personal
- Mention how you know them
- Offer an incentive

Your Book Blurb

- 200 words
- Use 4–5 bullet point benefits
- Create a call to action

> TITLE
> Introduction
> Body of your pitch
> Bullet points
> Conclusion
> Call to action

Your Testimonial Email

- Include a rating system.
- Ask for a short testimonial.
- Be personal.

> Hi NAME,
> State what you have done and why.
> Ask politely for a testimonial for your book.
> Thank them in advance.
> Use a personal sign off.

Outlining Your Wiki Page

Publishing a Wikipedia page can be tricky, so you have create one and have it edited by a Wikipedia editor, streamlining it for public use. Queue up your media mentions, and remember to not be salesy or narcissistic in your writing—facts only.

1 day

To create your Wikipedia page for publicity/media relations

Keep in mind that if you cannot get this right or you do not have the time, you should hire someone off Elance or Upwork (formerly Odesk) to do it for you. You can have it done for $50–$100 in one day, and the result will be excellently done by a Wikipedia professional.

- Use an alias.
- Find credible sources on large websites.
- Review at least 10 Wikipedia pages from other authors.
- Review the Wikipedia guidelines and rules in detail.
- The average Wikipedia page is 500 words long.

Your Wikipedia Entry

Create your Wikipedia entry in this box, and start by answering these questions:

Who are you?
Where are you from?
What are you best known for? (notables)

What awards have you won?
What products have you invented?
What companies do you own?

Write a paragraph about your early life.
Who were your parents?
What were your early life inspirations?

Write a paragraph about your education and early career.
Where did you study?
What was your process of becoming an expert?

Detail any key years where notables happened.
Have you published any books?
Have you done any collaborations?
Have you had any TV or magazine appearances?

Write a paragraph about your personal life.
Outline any awards.

Add an extensive bibliography to back up each claim using media sources.

Your SEO Strategy Map

SEO is the lifeblood of marketing online, and you need to understand it to get ahead. Read the two suggested resources in your guide, and then fill in the sheets below. A straightforward SEO strategy map outlines the keywords you will use in different types of media content. This content will attract traffic for you over time.

1 day

Discover influencers that will endorse your book.

Discovered Niche Keywords

- Find 2 lead keywords (long tail keywords)
- Find 6 main keywords (medium–high competition)
- Find 12 secondary keywords (low competition)

*Take note: Google Keyword Research Tool is no longer available. Instead, I highly recommend using a paid keyword platform like WordTracker to discover relevant keyword terms simply and easily.

Lead Keywords			
1		2	
Main Keywords			
3		6	
4		7	
5		8	
Secondary Keywords			
9		15	
10		16	
11		17	
12		18	
13		19	
14		20	

SEO Strategy Map

Each platform requires one lead keyword, 1–2 main keywords, and 3–4 secondary keywords.

Platform		Lead keywords	Main keywords	Secondary keywords
1	Amazon			
2	Lulu			
3	Clickbank			
4	Smashwords			
5	Payloadz			
6	Book website			
7	Blog			
8	Sales page (microsites)			
9	Facebook			
10	Twitter			
11	YouTube			
12	LinkedIn			
13	Pinterest			
14	Wikipedia			
15	Google+			

Aim for a keyword density of 2–3% in every piece of content that you create. To create your meta details, use a tool like this one here: *http://tools.seobook.com/meta-medic/*

The Press Release List

A lot of what makes your press release great is a high-impact headline. Here you will create your newsworthy headline, and then you will outline your post. Finally, you will publish this press release on a few PR websites to get the word out by creating a PR list.

 1 day

 Create 3–5 powerful versions of your press release.

Headline and press releases require keyword integration!

> Your powerful headline here:

When journalists search to share news, they will assess your headline most critically. Spend 50% of your time creating the ideal headline to improve the virality of your news.

Your Press Release Body Copy

> Start writing your press release here:
>
> Date, city, and strong lead-in sentence that grabs the reader's attention
>
> The introductory paragraph describing what news has happened
> This paragraph must summarize the entire press release succinctly.
>
> The facts of the story
> Remember, this is news, not sales.
> (Answer the who, what, when, where, and how.)
>
> Give the reader a reason to care about this news.
> Add your viral element. (Why is this worth sharing?)
>
> Link to your book

Press Release Date & Time Selection

Once your press releases are complete, you need quality news sources to share them with. I encourage you to find at least 15 PR websites or local publications for your campaign. Conduct research online, and build a list for yourself.

1 day

To build a reusable list of PR sites and outlets and to establish accounts

	Press Release Sites	Account Login Details	Fees
1	iNewswire		
2	Newswiretoday		
3	24-7 Press Release		
4	1888PressRelease		
5	ClickPress		
6	PR.com		
7	EcommWire		
8	Express-Press-Release		
9	PR-Inside		
10	PRUrgent.com		
11	PRlog.com		
12	PressMethod.com		
13	PR9.com		
14	Local newspaper		
15	Local newspaper		
16	HARO		

THE ONLINE SALES INFRASTRUCTURE BLUEPRINT

"Never forget that you only have one opportunity to make a first impression—with investors, with customers, with PR, and with marketing."
NATALIE MASSENET

As the lead marketer for your own book, you need to know how to build a powerful online sales infrastructure, or funnel, to create sales. This means knowing how to attract and direct traffic and how to put together small-scale strategies that can be expanded as needed.

Each of your platforms will require infrastructure, or the basics that will allow you to sell there successfully. Focus most of your attention on your top three platforms and top three goals.

The Website Strategy Exercise

Your website and blog can and should be integrated if you are starting off on a small scale, to consolidate your traffic and resources. You need to build a quick website strategy to make sure that as you design, or have it designed, it turns out well.

 1 day

 *To build a reusable list of PR sites and outlets and to establish accounts*

- Find 5 other author websites that you like, and take note of the structure.
- Create your content/navigation outline (menu systems).
- Find a template that will work with your outline.
- Customize the template, or pay to have it customized for you.

Use this five-page plan to create your website quickly and easily, or hand this to a WordPress developer that you find on a website like Themeforest.com. There you can buy a website for $30–$50 and have it set up for you for $200.

The Website Strategy

Your Website Name:	
Your Website Menu System & Content	
	Home
	About
	Book/Buy
	Blog
	Contact

Must-Have WordPress Plugins (Functionality):

Easydigitaldownloads Plugin

Website Color Scheme:

Starting Blog Content Titles:

1	
2	
3	
4	
5	
6	
7	
8	
9	
10	

WordPress Login Details

WordPress Developer's Details:

Building Lead Generation Packs

A lead generation pack consists of a strong sales pitch for your book wrapped in a description that you can use on your top three third-party sales sites. It also consists of your professional book and author images, your blurb, endorsements, and testimonials.

On each platform, you will make sure that you use these to their optimal impact.

1 day

Upload your lead generation pack to each third-party seller website.

- Find 5 other author websites that you like, and take note of the structure.
- Create your content/navigation outline (menu systems).
- Find a template that will work with your outline.
- Customize the template, or pay to have it customized for you.

Use this five-page plan to create your website quickly and easily, or hand this to a WordPress developer that you find on a website like Themeforest.com. There you can buy a website for $30–$50 and have it set up for you for $200.

Clickbank.com Pack	Check
Login:	
1 Powerful, short book description with keywords	
2 Strong Clickbank sales page/landing page	
3 Book and author images	
4 Microsite (mini one-page website)	
5 Endorsements	
6 Testimonials	
7 Blurb	
8 Keyword integration for all copy	

Lulu.com Pack	Check
Login:	
1	Powerful, short book description with keywords	
2	Strong Clickbank sales page/landing page	
3	Book and author images	
4	Microsite (mini one-page website)	
5	Endorsements	
6	Testimonials	
7	Blurb	
8	Keyword integration for all copy	

Payloadz.com Pack	Check
Login:	
1	Powerful, short book description with keywords	
2	Strong Clickbank sales page/landing page	
3	Book and author images	
4	Microsite (mini one-page website)	
5	Endorsements	
6	Testimonials	
7	Blurb	
8	Keyword integration for all copy	

Assets for Your Social Funnel

DAY 17

Use these handy checklists to make sure that you have all the content assets available for you when you set up your social selling platforms.

1 day

Sign up for social accounts, and establish identity there with content.

Basic Content Asset Pack for Social Media

The one-liner and single paragraph you created earlier can double as your short description and longer paragraph description if you do not want to make them unique.

1	3 x profile pictures of the author	
2	6 book images	
3	Initial 10 blog post links	
4	Powerful short description (50 words)	
5	Longer "about" description with keywords	

Facebook Page		Checklist
	Account Name:	
	Password:	
1	1 x profile image	
2	1 x cover image	
3	1 x call to action link to your book's website or microsite	
4	10 x blog post links as FB updates	
5	1 x short description	
6	1 x long description	

Twitter Page		Checklist
	Account Name:	
	Password:	
1	1 x profile image	
2	1 x cover image	
3	1 background image	
4	10 x blog post tweets and links	
5	1 x short Twitter description	
6	1 x outgoing link to book website	
Pinterest Page		Checklist
	Account Name:	
	Password:	
1	1 x profile image	
2	1 x outgoing link to website	
3	3 x boards with curated 6 images each	
4	10 x blog post links as images	
5	10 Pinterest keywords for description	
6	Follow 100 relevant people	
LinkedIn Page		Checklist
	Account Name:	
	Password:	
1	1 x profile image	
2	1 x background cover image	
3	1 x link to your book website	
4	10 x blog post links as published materials	
5	1 x short description	
6	1 x long description	
Google+ Page		Checklist
	Account Name:	
	Password:	
1	1 x profile image	
2	1 x cover image	
3	1 x link to your book website	
4	10 x blog post links as Google+ updates	
5	1 x short description	
6	1 x long description	

Content Requirements for Sales

DAY
18

During this setup process, you will be required to create a high impact sales landing page for your book. The better your sales writing, the higher your conversions!

- Research sales writing (check out Dan Kennedy).
- Be open, honest, and transparent.
- Use your lead generation pack (endorsements, testimonials, blurb).
- Long form sales letters are 3000 words or more.
- Short form sales letters are 1000 words or less.
- Create powerful headings and subheadings.
- Use video, audio, and copy to sell.
- Create strong calls to action.

1 day

Create a powerful sales page.

Short Form Sales Letter Template

Power headline with a buyer benefit

Author photo

Personalized, friendly introduction

Book images

Add an endorsement or two from experts.

Identify your buyer's problem.
Provide the solution to that problem in your book.
Help them understand your credentials.

Book images

List the benefits in bullet points (or use blurb).

Add your testimonials as social proof.

Offer them your book with a call to action.
Add a guarantee.

Book images

Provide a warning, and inject scarcity.
Close with a reminder.

Author photo

Personal sign off

The YouTube Strategy Exercise

DAY 19

Video and audio media sell more books; that is a fact. You need to set up a YouTube account so that you can take advantage of YouTube traffic from videos and podcasts. Sign up to YouTube; then create your first talking head video.

1 day

YouTube setup and 2-minute video introduction.

- Use the YouTube keyword tool to research keywords on this platform.

YouTube Page	Checklist
Account Name:	
Password:	
1 1 x profile image	
2 1 x background cover image	
3 all links to your book websites	
4 10 x blog posts converted into slideshow/audio videos	
5 1 x talking head introduction video	
6 1 x brief description	

Your Talking Head Video

- 2 hours maximum to film
- 1 cell phone or web camera
- Slow down how you speak.
- Write 2 pages of dialogue.

Talking Head Script: 2 Minutes

Author Introduction

Book one liner

Book paragraph explanation

A few benefits of reading the book

Some background on your personal story

A call to action prompt to buy your book

Using Fiverr

To convert your blog posts into audio videos with text and/or images, sign up to Fiverr to hire a voice over artist to do it for under $20 per video.

The Amazon Strategy Exercise

It is time to set up your Amazon bookseller's page. To do this, you need to get some strategic elements right and to keep your account information safe. Use these assets to create a powerful Amazon page, where you will sell lots of books.

1 day

Amazon page set up and optimization for sales

Amazon Page		Checklist
	Account Name:	
	Password:	
1	6 x book images	
2	1 x author photo	
3	Book blurb	
4	Book endorsements (and editorial reviews)	
5	Book testimonials	
6	1 x book description	
7	1 x author biography	

Your Author Biography

- Name
- Major published works
- Awards
- Credentials
- 50 words maximum

Start writing here:

THE
SOCIAL SALES
FUNNEL
BLUEPRINT

*"With the creation of Web 2.0, we are seeing
the emergence of a new type of digital consumer,
who is no longer simply a passive 'site-seer' on
a fixed consumer journey but an independent
explorer craving freedom, adventure and
companionship. The challenge for businesses
and advertisers is to engage with the active
digitraveller as well as the passive digitourist."*
SARAH MORNING

Social media exists in marketing to create conversions,
spur virality, and attract traffic to your core sales pages and
campaigns. You can use your social sales funnel to push traffic
to your top sales platforms to get those vital conversions.

The trick is to know how to manage your social media in a
scalable, sensible manner. You want fans and community
members to cross over and buy your book. This section of
your workbook will show you how you can get this done.

The Twitter Strategy Exercise

On Twitter, you will create daily tweets that will help you build a community that will help you attract clicks to your book website and sales pages or blog. The goal is always to get more people into your core sales funnel.

 1 day

 Populate Twitter with valuable fans and content.

- Remember to use keywords in all Twitter posts.
- All tweets are 140 characters or less.
- Include a hashtag to build an index of relevant tweets.
- Get on author lists.

Weekly Facebook Strategy Content Pack: 25 posts per week		Checklist
1	5 x update and image posts	
2	5 x update and video posts	
3	5 x update and blog link posts	
4	5 x image and book insight posts	
5	5 x marketing messages	

Each Facebook update should be between 50 and 150 characters in length. Some can be longer, but shorter messages tend to pack a punch. Create them below.

Daily Facebook Strategy Content Pack: 5 posts per day		Post Creation
1	1 x update and image post	
2	1 x update and video post	
3	1 x update and blog link post	
4	1 x image and book insight post	
5	1 x marketing message	

Facebook Strategy Outreach		Checklist
1	2–5 x educated comments on related pages per day	
2	Free copy of book to a fan every 2 weeks to collect testimonial	

The Facebook Strategy Exercise

On Twitter, you will create daily tweets that will help you build a community that will help you attract clicks to your book website and sales pages or blog. The goal is always to get more people into your core sales funnel.

 1 day

 *Populate Twitter with valuable fans and content.*

- Remember to use keywords in all Twitter posts.
- All tweets are 140 characters or less.
- Include a hashtag to build an index of relevant tweets.
- Get on author lists.

Weekly Twitter Strategy Content Pack: 50 tweets per week		Checklist
1	1 x tip tweet with blog link	
2	1 x quote tweet with third party link	
3	1 x insight/stat tweet, no link	
4	1 x response tweet to influencer	
5	1 x general niche tweet with hashtag	
6	1 x general niche tweet with hashtag	
7	1 x related author/book tweet with link	
8	1 x related author/book tweet with link	
9	1 x direct sales tweet	
10	1 x direct sales tweet	

Build your book hashtag; then use it in all book-related posts.

Hashtag: (Example: #TheMoneyBook)

Each Twitter update should be about 140 characters in length. Some can be shorter, and always shorten your URL. Create them below.

Daily Twitter Strategy Content Pack: 10 posts per day		Post Creation
1	1 x tip tweet with blog link	
2	1 x quote tweet with third party link	
3	1 x insight/stat tweet, no link	
4	1 x response tweet to influencer	
5	1 x general niche tweet with hashtag	
6	1 x general niche tweet with hashtag	
7	1 x related author/book tweet with link	
8	1 x related author/book tweet with link	
9	1 x direct sales tweet	
10	1 x direct sales tweet	

Twitter Strategy Extras

Twitter Strategy Outreach		Checklist
1	1–3 retweets per day	
2	2 Vine video tweets per week	
3	Follow 5 relevant fans a day	

The Pinterest Strategy Exercise

You need to get some images on your Pinterest page so that it can start driving traffic to your websites and sales pages. To do this, you need to post daily.

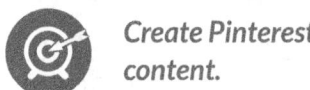

1 day

Create Pinterest content.

- Remember to use keywords in all pins.
- Create 5 different boards to begin with, and post each relevant image on the corresponding board.

Weekly Pinterest Strategy Content Pack: 20 posts per week, 1 video	Checklist
1 5 x tutorial image with link	
2 5 x book-related Instagram photo with quote and link	
3 5 x social author photo with link	
4 5 x book graphic with link	
5 1 x book blog related video with link	

Name Your Pinterest Boards

1	
2	
3	
4	
5	

Each Pinterest update should be less than 140 characters in length. Some can be longer, but keep readability in mind. Create them below.

Daily Pinterest Strategy Content Pack: 5 pins per day		Post Creation
1	1 x tutorial image with link	
2	1 x book-related Instagram photo with quote and link	
3	1 x social author photo with link	
4	1 x book graphic with link	
5	1 x book blog related video with link	

Pinterest Strategy Extras

Pinterest Strategy Outreach		Checklist
1	Re-pin 5 relevant images per day	
2	Comment on 2 pins each day	
3	Follow 5 people each day	

The LinkedIn Strategy Exercise

Your LinkedIn strategy will get you the best endorsements, recommendations, testimonials, and social proof for your marketing materials. Sharing content here is key.

 1 day

 *Create LinkedIn content.*

- Remember to use keywords in all updates.
- SP conversion stands for social proof conversion, or getting a contact to create an endorsement for you.

Weekly LinkedIn Strategy Content Pack: 15 posts per week		Checklist
1	3 x group responses with SP conversion	
2	3 x group responses with SP conversion	
3	3 x group responses with SP conversion	
4	3 x blog posts with link to website	
5	3 x shared third party posts	

LinkedIn Blog Reposting

You can repost your blog articles on LinkedIn to share with a wider community and to encourage clicks to your website. This is recommended at least three times a week.

Post Titles:

1	
2	
3	
4	
5	

Each LinkedIn group response needs to be highly personal and insightful and created in real time. Create them below.

Daily LinkedIn Strategy Content Pack: 3 responses per day, 1 blog post, 1 third-party blog link to share		Post Creation
1	1 x group responses with SP conversion	
2	1 x group responses with SP conversion	
3	1 x group responses with SP conversion	
4	1 x blog post with link to website	
5	1 x shared third party post	

LinkedIn Strategy Extras

LinkedIn Strategy Outreach		Checklist
1	Join 5–10 groups, and focus your efforts	
2	Make 5 relevant connections each day	
3	Email contacts for SP when a relationship has been established for a while	

The Google+ Exercise

Google+ is a great traffic generator, and it pays to post there. Focus on influencers instead of fans to build a better reputation for yourself and your book.

- Remember to use keywords in all updates.
- Use different images from the ones you use on FB and Twitter.

1 day

Create Google+ content.

Weekly Google+ Strategy Content Pack: 15 posts per week, 1 Hangout video		Checklist
1	5 x book image & discussion point	
2	5 x general image & story/experience	
3	5 x image & marketing message	
4	1 x hangout video	

Google+ Blog Links

You can post blog links on Google+ to attract readers to your website and to get more sales. This is recommended at least three times a week.

Post Titles:

1	
2	
3	

Each Google+ post needs to be properly categorized with selected keywords. These posts can be between 50–200 words long. Create them below.

Daily Google+ Strategy Content Pack: 3 updates, 1 Hangout video	Post Creation
1	1 x book image & discussion point	
2	1 x general image & story/experience	
3	1 x image & marketing message	
4	1 x Google Hangout video	

Google+ Strategy Extras

Google+ Strategy Outreach	Checklist
1	Comment on influencer posts twice daily	
2	Create circles with segmented groups	
3	Message circle members for SP	

The Analytics Strategy Exercise

 *1 day*

It is time to establish your account on Hootsuite so that you can monitor and measure the progress of your social media posts. Then you will be able to tweak them for better clicks, responses, growth, and sales.

 *Sign up for Hootsuite, and establish your social media analytics dashboard.*

Hootsuite pulls in different social media data so that it can be effectively tracked and analyzed holistically for a competent social media strategy. You will need to add your social media accounts one by one and give Hootsuite permission to access your data.

Hootsuite Package		Checklist
	Account Name:	
	Password:	
1	Add your Facebook page	
2	Add your Twitter page	
3	Add your LinkedIn page	
4	Add your Pinterest page	
5	Add your YouTube page	
6	Add your Google+ page	
7	Add your Instagram page	

Once your account is established, check on your analytics every three days. Take note of which posts outperform others and why. Always write it down and implement changes.

Compile an analytics insight report for yourself at the end of each week. This is to give you actionable changes for the new week!

Weekly Report:

1	Facebook Report	
2	Twitter Report	
3	LinkedIn Report	
4	Pinterest Report	
5	YouTube Report	
6	Google+ Report	
7	Instagram Report	

THE
BOOK BLOG
BLUEPRINT

"Don't try to plan everything out to the very last detail. I'm a big believer in just getting it out there: create a minimal viable product or website, launch it, and get feedback."
NEIL PATEL

Your book's blog should be a cross between highly interesting subjects surrounding your book and a place where fans can come to learn more about you. Running your traffic through your blog allows you to directly convert visitors into buyers.

That is why your blog may be the most important location for your marketing efforts online, especially if you plan to write books in the future. The more content you publish, the higher your traffic and community numbers will get.

Blog Launch Essentials

Launching a blog or a website with a blogroll on it is challenging. A blog exists for many important marketing reasons. The larger your readership there, the more books you will sell over time, so it pays to keep it populated with content.

Your blog should be launched with 10 SEO posts that you have created. Outline them below, and ready them for publication. Each post should be 500–1000 words.

Create catchy titles for each of your 10 core blog posts here. You can also choose to launch with 30 posts or keep 20 aside to post daily in real time.

1 day

To launch a successful blog

Blog Content Launch	Checklist
1	
2	
3	
4	
5	
6	
7	
8	
9	
10	

What Goes Into a Blog Post?

	Blog Post Structure
1	Title
2	Introductory Paragraph
3	Subheading
4	Body Text
5	Subheading
6	Body Text
7	Subheading Body Text
8	3 x Images spread throughout post
9	A video (potentially)
10	Conclusion/Call to Action for Engagement

Blog Launch Extras

	Launch Extras	Checklist
1	Announce your launch on social media.	
2	Create a competition to attract awareness.	
3	Share each blog post on your SM pages.	
4	Bookmark each post on StumbleUpon.	
5	Add a "Buy Now" button to your blog.	

Traffic Generation Exercise

Here you will establish your foundation pack of content and implement some blog strategies that spark traffic generation and can kick start book sales.

 *1 day*

Take a close look at your 10–30 blog post titles. Practice converting these into social media posts that hook the reader and prompt a click, with a strong call to action.

 *Convert blog post content into usable social media posts.*

- Keyword optimization at 2% is required.

Blog Post Titles	Social Media Hooks
Example: How to Grow an Herb Garden	Do your herbs keep dying? Here's how to grow them the old fashioned way. Click to read!
1	
2	
3	
4	
5	
6	
7	
8	
9	
10	
11	
12	
13	
14	
15	

Blog Post Titles	Social Media Hooks
Example: How to Grow an Herb Garden	Do your herbs keep dying? Here's how to grow them the old fashioned way. Click to read!
16	
17	
18	
19	
20	

Conducting Community Research

Perfecting your community checklist is key to attracting long-term blog readers. Make sure you run through this checklist to get it done.

Find ten competitors with similar topics around your blog and book.

1 day

Conduct community research, and make it easy for them to come back.

Competitors	URL
1	
2	
3	
4	
5	
6	
7	
8	
9	
10	

For each competitor, fill in the following areas:

Competitor	Core topics	Reader numbers	Posts with the most comments	Best types of post	Most shared	CTAs
Ex.: The Rea Herb Blog	Growing	18,560	Plant identification	Lists	Video posts	Copy calls to action here.
1						
2						
3						
4						
5						
6						
7						
8						
9						
10						

Use this checklist to tweak the extras:

Community Extras		Checklist
1	Check readability of post.	
2	Use first person speech.	
3	Look at your reader conversion.	
4	Call for subscribers.	
5	Offer a 20% discount off your book for new subscribers.	
6	Reply to all comments and emails.	

The Blog Content Strategy Exercise

DAY 30

Here is where you will shape your blog content strategy. Test which types of posts people like, and work on creating more of them. You need to establish what to post and when for maximum impact.

1 day, ongoing

Build a blog content strategy

Fill in the following to establish your content strategy:

Blog Content Strategy Substance > Workflow > Governance > Structure	
Content Components: Substance (What topics will your blog explore?)	
Content Components: Structure (What types of post will you use? Add them to this list.)	
List	
How-to	
Interview	
Expert	
Influencer	
Review	
Showcase	
Video	
Image	
Audio	

People Components: Workflow (Who will research, SEO, write, edit, publish, and promote the posts daily?)	

People Components: Governance (Who will respond to all posts and for how much time each day?)	

Decide at what time your posts will go live, and note the response.

Time to Post		
Title	Time Posted	Response

The Guest Blogger List

There is no better way to attract attention to yourself online than to make friends with other bloggers. Having other experts post on your book website is key to traffic generation and sales!

 *1 day, ongoing*

 *Create a guest blogger list.*

Find 10 other relevant expert bloggers online, and record their details.

Guest Blogger Outreach	
Name	**Email**
1	
2	
3	
4	
5	
6	
7	
8	
9	
10	

Create your standard guest blog email below using the outline:

Hi NAME,

This is where I know you from.
This is what I would like from you and why.

This is my website where the post will go.
This is the incentive I can offer you if you guest post on my blog.

A warm sign off,
Your personal name and email

Key Metrics Analysis Exercise

Blog analytics are more complex than social media analytics. You need to sign up to Google Webmaster Tools to get Google Analytics. From there, establish metrics goals for your first month—then break them down into micro goals and segment where you will get your traffic from using your social sales funnel and advertising.

1 day, ongoing

Sign up to Google Analytics, and establish metrics goals.

Google Analytics		Checklist
	Account Name:	
	Password:	
1	Use Google Analytics plugin for WordPress.	
2	Place your generated website code in this area.	
3	You will see your data over time.	

Establishing Metrics Goals

Set your goals for each metric, and try to reach these goals within a specific timeframe. For example, with 40,000 total site visits a month to your microsite, with a 3% conversion rate—that means 3% of your 40,000 visitors will buy your book. That is 1,200 sales! It will take time to build up this traffic flow and to get this conversion rate.

Key Performance Indicators		Goal
Main Goal: Sell more books		3% landing page conversion rate
1	Total site visits	
2	Page views	
3	Average time spent on site	
4	New visits	
5	Bounce rate	
6	Keyword efficiency	

Test posts with Optimizely.

Optimizely is a website testing tool where you can split your traffic and see which version of a blog post does better. Use this tool to perfect your posts by signing up for it.

Optimizely Login		Checklist
	Account Name:	
	Password:	

THE
BLOG OUTREACH STRATEGY BLUEPRINT

"The Blogger Outreach Equation sets the foundation for establishing mutually beneficial relationships around content publishers care about: timely, engaging, and new information that speaks to their audience."

KELSEY LIBERT

Your blog is a critical part of your marketing strategy, but beyond the content you will post, there is a myriad of outreach tactics that you need to get right. A strong outreach strategy gets you fans and a larger community that you can sell to.

Understanding how to execute a competent blog outreach strategy is what this section of your workbook is all about. Here you will begin your hunt for the biggest audience possible.

The Influencer Strategy Exercise

Find the main influencers in your niche, and figure out a method of approaching them or befriending them. It is hard, but it can do wonders for your traffic!

NB! Influencers are contacted by bloggers and authors all the time. Key influencers can get as many as 100 emails in their box every day with requests. You have to make it easy.

1 day, ongoing

Build an influencer list, and create your influencer email.

Influencer Outreach List	
Name	**Email**
1	
2	
3	
4	
5	
6	
7	
8	
9	
10	

When the influencer gets your mail, they will know who you are and that you have been helping them for some time. They will be far more likely to help you now. Use this basic email template to approach them for a post or an endorsement.

Hi NAME,

This is where I know you from.
This is what I would like from you and why.

This is my website where the post will go.
This is the incentive I can offer you if you guest post on my blog.

A warm sign off,
Your personal name and email

The Link Building List

DAY
34

Whenever you leave a comment on another person's blog or website, it translates as a white hat link for your website. Comment enough, and you will build up link power for your website. Make sure all websites you comment on are 100% relevant to your book and niche.

1 day, ongoing

Sign up to Bitly, and record where you comment.

Sign up for a Bitly account to shorten and track the links you will use in your comments.

Bitly Account		Checklist
	Account Name:	
	Password:	

Identify 5–10 blog posts a day to comment on:

	Blog Post URL	Check
1		
2		
3		
4		
5		
6		
7		
8		
9		
10		

The Expert–Platform Connection

It is not easy to befriend an influencer. These are people that get hundreds of mails daily, and they can choose whom to help and whom to ignore. Reaching out to them as a stranger will always get you ignored. Here is how to change that!

 1 day

 To create an influencer strategy that works

The Influencer Strategy Checklist

How do you get on the radar of a niche influencer? By diverting your attention to their marketing for a while. Become a super fan, and they will notice you. Follow these steps:

	Influencer Strategy Checklist	Check
1	Like, follow, and subscribe to the influencer's blog.	
2	Dedicate 1–2 weeks to sharing their media specifically.	
3	Share or comment on their FB posts daily.	
4	Strike up a worthwhile conversation on Twitter about their work.	
5	Engage them on a LinkedIn group.	
6	Share their pins and Instagram shots.	
7	Engage in discussion on their Google+ posts.	
8	Encourage others to read their blog.	
9	Encourage others to buy their books and products.	
10	Create a blog post honoring them.	
11	Comment thoughtfully on their blog.	
12	At the end of the 2-week period, send your email.	

The Endorsement Strategy Exercise

Aim for expert or celebrity endorsements to skyrocket sales. These can be custom written, or you can make it easier for the pro by offering them some options.

Find your expert linchpin! Who among everyone in your niche is the most respected or most popular online?

 *1 day*

 Find five amazing endorsements for your book.

> Add their name and contact details here:

Apply your influencer strategy to securing this "whale" endorsement; then you can use it to secure the other four or 10—whatever you can manage.

Celebrities & Expert Influencers	Email
1	
2	
3	
4	
5	
6	
7	
8	
9	
10	

Once your linchpin expert is secured, add their endorsement to your query email.

Hi NAME,

This is where I know you from.
TOP EXPERT X gave me this about my book [include endorsement]...
This is what I would like from you and why.

This is my website where the post will go.
This is the incentive I can offer you if you endorse my book.

A warm sign off,
Your personal name and email

If you find it useful, you can simply mention the names of a few experts who have endorsed you as you send out more query emails.

The Authenticity Exercise

DAY 37

Authenticity and reputation matter when you sell books online. That is why these quality control measures must be put in place to keep your blog and online presence governed correctly. Run through this checklist to ensure your reputation is safe.

1 day

Perform these strategies to maintain quality and authenticity online.

	Quality Checklist	Check
1	Be honest and fair in all online communication.	
2	Never get into fights with anyone online, ever.	
3	Focus on appearing everywhere—be a guest blogger!	
4	Attend book fairs, events, and writing conferences.	
5	Host book signings, and share the images on social media.	
6	Ensure all content you create goes through an editor first.	
7	Edit for grammar, fact-checking, spelling, and entertainment value.	
8	Be yourself on social media.	
9	Create a social media policy guide.	
10	Use news sites to "make the news" as often as you can.	
11	Always respond to your fans.	

Designing a Blog Tour

Here you will prepare the email you need to set up a blog tour, which can include multiple locations online where you want to appear as a guest author.

1 day

Design a blog tour.

First, decide which tour platforms you will visit.

	Blog Tour Locations	Check
1	Guest posting on a popular third-party blog	
2	Cohosting a Twitter chat	
3	Cohosting a Facebook chat	
4	Appearing live in a Facebook group Q&A	
5	Guest appearances on popular YouTube feeds	
6	Hosting a Reddit chat	
7	Appearing in an audio podcast	
8	Appearing as an expert guest in a LinkedIn group	
9	Hosting a Google+ Hangout	
10	Engaging in a rapid-fire Google+ discussion	
11	Providing infographic images to other bloggers	

Next, use your influencer and guest blogger list to set up a series of dates and times, filling them slot by slot until you have a full month of daily blog tour appearances.

	Blog Tour Locations	Timeslot	Date
1			
2			
3			
4			
5			
6			
7			
8			
9			
10			

To do this, create an email explaining your book blog tour briefly and inviting your network to be part of it. Be sure to mention endorsements and incentives to be taken seriously!

Hi NAME,

This is where I know you from.
TOP EXPERT X gave me this about my book [include endorsement]...

I am hosting a book tour and would like to include a stop with you on [platform] on [date] at [timeslot]. Would this be possible, or can we arrange a time that suits you?

Here are the benefits for you [include incentives].

I look forward to your response.

A warm sign off,
Your personal name and email

Make sure that you show up for every scheduled appearance and leave a lasting impression behind so that many of these individuals invite you back!

THE
AUDIO SALES
BLUEPRINT

"Audio content has a distinct advantage: Audio is "eyes free" content."

RUSS HENNEBERRY

There is one straightforward way to increase your sales right from the beginning. In the world of book lovers, there are some that do not like to read or cannot find the time to do it. That is why selling an audio version of your book is a huge advantage.

Then your book can be enjoyed while performing another task, which makes it functional and interesting. Broaden your target market with an audio book strategy, and you will snag a portion of the market that is largely untapped.

The Outsourcing List

It is time to get your audio book created, which means that you need to outsource this critical job to someone that can do it well. Here is a list of the best places.

1 day

Locate the right individual or company to convert your book into an audio file.

	Outsourcer/Freelancer List	Checklist
1	Elance.com	
2	Guru.com	
3	Freelancer.com	
4	Upwork.com	
5	Fiverr.com	
6	Get quotes from local companies.	
7	Get quotes from international companies.	
8	Use a service like voicebunny.com.	

To identify the right person, follow these rules:

Rules for Freelancer Selection	
1	A complete portfolio of proven samples
2	A full past client list
3	Client testimonials and endorsements that are verified
4	Before hiring them, chat with them on IM to test communication ability.
5	Give them a sample piece of audio to complete first (1 page).
6	Chat to them on the telephone.
7	Establish clear deadlines.
8	Establish clear, fixed payment terms (not hourly).
9	Be clear in your instructions.
10	Review the audio a third way through, then halfway, and then complete.

The iTunes Page Checklist

The next step is to set up your iTunes page, where you will be selling your audio book. iTunes can bring in just as much revenue as Amazon if you set it up correctly.

- Remember to include keywords in all content.

1 day

Set up your iTunes page for sales.

iTunes Page		Checklist
	Account Name:	
	Password:	
1	7 x book images, 1 with audio discs	
2	1 x author photo	
3	Book blurb for description	
4	Book endorsements (and editorial reviews)	
5	Book testimonials	
6	A full sales description	
7	1 x author biography	
8	Hire freelancers to add in 5–10 5-star reviews of your book.	

The iTunes Strategy Exercise

How do you market your new audio book on iTunes? By creating and packaging snippets of audio and coupling them with strong graphics and copy.

- Speak to your freelancer about creating your snippets.

 1 day

 Create iTunes content for marketing.

Your iTunes Marketing Pack		Checklist
1	5 minutes of dynamic audio snippet for reader testing	
2	3–5 short audio books around your core book topic (20 minutes each)	
3	A full-length audio book for free with advertising inside it	
4	10% off promotion for your audio book version	
5	Post about your audio books on social media.	
6	Find related audio books, and leave a link to yours there.	
7	Always include a link to your audio book on sales pages.	
8	Send influencers/guests a sample chapter in audio.	

You will also need to have a specially created image made to complement your book images. Your book cover will need to be placed on discs or CDs for the iTunes audience.

iTunes Book-Disc Images	
	1 x book and disc with a realistic image
	1 x close-up disc with book branding on it
	1 x author photo holding discs with headphones on

The Audio Strategy Exercise

DAY

42

Marketing audio outside of iTunes can be a challenge but not when you have a strategy in place. Knowing where to sell and how is half the battle.

1 day

Consider the additional costs and time required to create unique audio packs. Also be sure to select the right audio formats and provider.

Create an audio strategy, and locate audio markets.

Audio Book Marketing Pack	Provider	Cost	Time	Format
1 3 x audio book images				
2 Audio book sales letter (short)				
3 Audio book snippets				
4 Audio book sample				
5 Audio book endorsements				
6 Audio book reviews				
7 Audio book author bio				

Once this is done, you can move on to building your comprehensive audio book list. Find platforms online where you can sell your audio book. Here are some to get you started:

Audio Book Platform List

Audio Bookseller's List		Checklist
1	iTunes	
2	Amazon	
3	Pandora	
4	Rhapsody	
5	MySpace	
6	CDBaby	
7	Emusic	
8	YouTube	
9		
10		
11		
12		
13		
14		
15		

The Audio Sales Blueprint

When you commit to selling audio, you should really be in the audio sphere, which means podcasting regularly. The more podcasts you make, the more listeners you will attract and the more audio books you will sell.

1 day

Establish a podcast, and build a podcast community.

Podcast Pack		Checklist
1	Pick a popular topic around your book.	
2	Create a name for your podcast.	
3	Create 5-minute monologue podcasts weekly.	
4	Partner with another blogger, and record a discussion.	
5	Interview another expert on your topic in audio.	
6	Create a dynamic podcast music intro for your show.	
7	Create teleclass tutorials that teach your audience.	
8	Build a 3- to 5-lesson audio series promoting your book.	
9	Appear on YouTube podcasts in person.	
10	Appear on popular existing podcasts in your niche.	

The goal here is downloads. You should place a "download podcast" or audio button on your blog, sales pages, and website too.

The Show Begins

Add in your first four show titles, the timeslot you will create and post for, the dates, and who will appear with you in the discussion.

	Podcast title	Date	Timeslot	Guest
1				
2				
3				
4				

To begin with four podcasts a month would be great. If you can manage more, then by all means do them. They attract a fair amount of traffic.

Managing Your Audio Sales

Managing your audio sales means that you may end up needing additional equipment and a greater investment in your audio book and podcasts.

 4 days

 *Build a small studio, and track your downloads.*

Professional Podcasting Equipment		Checklist
1	Audio software: Audacity	
2	Audio software: Adobe Audition	
3	Audio software: Skype	
4	Audio software: Levelator	
5	A condenser mic for quiet environments (USB input)	
6	A dynamic mic for directional audio (USB input)	
7	For multiple guests, a mixer is required.	
8	A portable recorder for interviews	
9	A quality set of headphones (with mic potentially)	
10	A mic stand	

When you start up, all you need is a good-quality webcam, but be warned, the audio quality will be hard to get right. When you start earning, you must upgrade your equipment.

An Audio Marketing Trick

At live events, take your portable recorder with you for on-the-spot interviews, endorsements, and reviews of your book. List each person's name and details—then package the audio and ping them when it is published for a boost in traffic and virality.

Live on the Portable Mic

Name	Email	Location
1		
2		
3		
4		
5		
6		
7		
8		
9		
10		

THE
YOUTUBE &
EMAIL BLUEPRINT

"The evolution of social media into a robust mechanism for social transformation is already visible. Despite many adamant critics who insist that tools like Facebook, Twitter, and YouTube are little more than faddish distractions useful only to exchange trivial information, these critics are being proven wrong time and again."

SIMON MAINWARING

YouTube is a marketing goldmine, and for the author marketers that are not afraid of stepping into the limelight, it is a great place to source traffic and build a professional reputation. YouTube and a good email list sell books in volumes if you know how to use them.

Many of the up-and-coming authors in the world are already on YouTube for this reason. They focus on putting out excellent, engaging content so that their fans and potential buyers always find their way back to key sales pages.

YouTube Description Training

Record your details here when setting up your new YouTube page. This is a little more difficult than other pages, and it requires close attention to SEO when you create your descriptions.

 1 day

 *Sign up for YouTube, and create your first SEO description.*

YouTube Page		Checklist
	Account Name:	
	Password:	
1	6 x book images	
2	1 x author photo	
3	Book blurb copy	
4	Book endorsements	
5	Book testimonials	
6	1 x book "about" copy	
7	1 x subscriber video & text	
8	Website and social & sales links	
9	1 x background graphic	

YouTube Description Creation:

- Include lead, main, and secondary keywords in your description.
- Describe the video in an exciting way (use a hook).
- Stick to the 5000-character limit.
- Include links to your other videos or pages.
- Optimize your video metadata with a strong title.

Based on your first talking head video, create your YouTube description below:

YouTube Video Training

DAY 50

Create your YouTube strategy, and try to stick to it. No other social media platform can escalate sales as rapidly as YouTube if you consistently post there.

- Remember to use keywords in all copy.

1 day

Create a YouTube sales strategy.

Monthly YouTube Strategy Content Pack: 14 videos per month	Checklist
1 8 x talking head videos	
2 1 x PowerPoint slide video	
3 1 x Google+ Hangouts video	
4 1 x event video	
5 1 x 20- to 30-second marketing ad video	
6 1 x branded stats video	
7 1 x niche video episode	

Carefully assemble your YouTube metadata for each video:

Title:

Description:

Keywords:

Call to action:

Each YouTube video should be about two minutes long for maximum virality. Longer videos (15 minutes) are great, but they are viewed less often. Devise your daily strategy below.

Daily YouTube Strategy Content Pack: 1 post per day Pick your type of video.		Hosted video URL
1	1 x talking head video	
2	1 x PowerPoint slide video	
3	1 x Google+ Hangouts video	
4	1 x event video	
5	1 x 20- to 30-second marketing ad video	
6	1 x branded stats video	
7	1 x niche video episode	
8	1 x podcast	

YouTube Strategy Extras

YouTube Strategy Outreach		Checklist
1	Subscribe to relevant YouTube feeds	
2	Comment on relevant YouTube feeds	
3	Form relationships with other YouTubers	

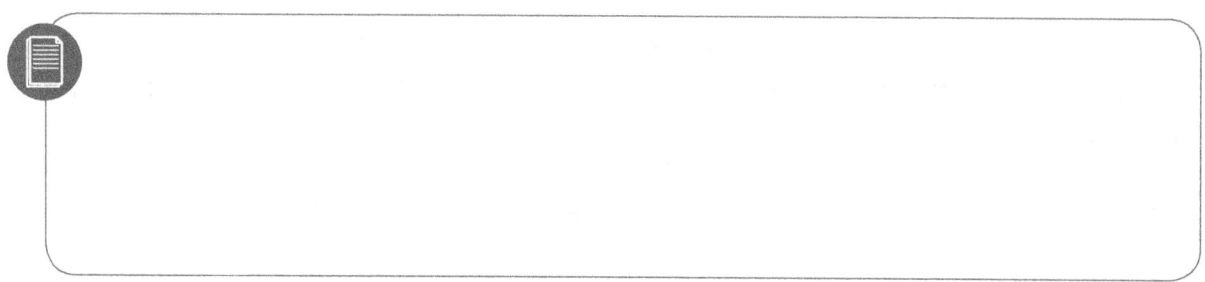

The Email Signature Checklist

Create your email signature using this handy checklist. Make sure that you do not include anything else as it could be a bad practice.

- Resist the urge to add sales links, spam, or quotes to your email signature!

 1 day

 Create a professional email signature.

Email Signature Checklist	Checklist
1	Core email should be from your main book website.	
2	Add your full name.	
3	Add your full title.	
4	Add your company name.	
5	Add your email and telephone contact details.	
6	Add your Skype or IM details.	
7	Only use a plain font (Times New Roman, Arial, Verdana).	
8	Stick to black and your business colors only.	
9	Make your signature readable in plain text.	
10	Add in a professional photo of yourself.	

Do not add a disclaimer to your email. They serve no purpose at all and are not legally binding. The goal of your email signature is to help people find out who you are; it is not to sell them your product.

Use the checklist above to create your email signature below:

> Start here:

Then use a free tool to convert your signature into HTML, such as https://htmlsig.com/.

The Email List Policy

Choose from a list of email providers, and begin to build your email list. This list will earn you a lot of money in the future and should be a priority sales asset for you.

 1 day

Compare some email providers by researching them to see which crucial services they offer, and then select one:

 Find an email provider, and begin a customer/fan email list.

Email Providers	Free	Monthly costs	Template access	Custom toresponders	Google Analytics	Split testing
1 Mailchimp						
2 GetResponse						
3 iContact						
4 AWeber						
5 Campaign Monitor						
6 Vertical Response						
7 Campaigner						
8 Benchmark Email						

Add a Mailchimp email signup plugin to your WordPress website. Create a short landing page on your website where people can be convinced to subscribe to your list.

Research and create your brief email list policy below. Start by reviewing Mailchimp's own privacy policy: http://mailchimp.com/legal/privacy/.

Build yours below using your own words:

Newsletter Promotion Strategy

DAY 53

In order to build your email list, you need to have a strong landing page that converts your traffic into subscribers. This copy has to be strong, so if you cannot get a decent conversion rate yourself, consider hiring a sales writer later on.

1 day

Create a professional email signature.

Create your 300- to 350-word email landing page copy below:

Email Landing Page:
Tell you readers what you want them to do in a step-by-step fashion.

[Headline]

Short 1- to 2-sentence problem presentation
Short 1 sentence solution offering

Benefits
A short description on what the list is about
A reassurance about spam and over-emailing (email list policy link)

A strong call to action pointing at an opt-in form

A warm sign off

Pick Your Free Giveaway:

Email Content Asset Options			
1	A sample chapter of your book	4	An e-course related to your book
2	A section of audio from your book	5	Entry into an exclusive competition
3	Short ebooks related to your book	6	A related guide

Email List Analytics Exercise

You have five days to orientate yourself in email list tracking and analysis. Improving your email sales technique during this time will get you more sales later on.

 *4 days*

 Build a small studio, and track your downloads.

Create and test each of these six core email types.

- Do not send your list more than six emails a month.

	Sales Email Selection	Checklist
1	Newsletter containing general & social news	
2	A dedicated email offer	
3	A digest (short form newsletter with lists and links)	
4	Lead email with valuable content, offers, and giveaways	
5	Sponsorship emails for other bloggers/authors	
6	Transactional emails	

Run an email campaign for five days by creating each mail, sending it – then analyzing the response by looking at these key metrics. Record your findings below.

	Email Analytics Report	Received mail	pened mail	Links clicked	Replies	Sales	Shares
1	Newsletter						
2	Dedicated sales email						
3	Digest						
4	Lead email						
5	Sponsorship email						
6	Transactional email						

Alternatively, you can focus on one type of email and split-test using a tool like Optimizely or the Mailchimp split-testing tool.

THE EVENT PROMOTION BLUEPRINT

"You see, it's never the environment; it's never the events of our lives, but the meaning we attach to the events-how we interpret them—that shapes who we are today and who we'll become tomorrow."

TONY ROBBINS

It is not enough to write a book and market it; you also need to be prepared to travel to showcase your book at events or to be a guest at one. Events have a unique way of getting the word out about who you are and the book you have written.

Making sure that you hit several events during a three-month marketing boom will increase your sales. The more appearances you can squeeze into your schedule, the better off you will be. Then your online sales funnel will really be working for you.

The Twitter Chat Exercise

Arrange a Twitter chat by filling in the details below and making the necessary arrangements. This chat needs to be promoted for a week or two before the event.

 1 day

 *Create a professional email signature.*

Step 1: Establish the Arrangements

Twitter Chat		
1	Chat Type:	
2	Chat Topic:	
3	Guest:	
4	Date:	
5	Time:	
6	Budget:	
7	Hashtag:	

Step 2: Promote Your Chat Event

Twitter Chat Promotion List		Checklist
1	Website announcement	
2	Blog post release	
3	Press release	
4	Facebook promotion	
5	Twitter promotion	
6	YouTube talking head clip	
7	LinkedIn group promotion	
8	Google+ promotion	
9	Influencer outreach	
10	Paid advertising to a budget	

The Google+ Hangouts Exercise

 1 day

 *To arrange your first Google+ Hangout with other bloggers and experts.*

Plan your Google Hangout by sending invites to the right people and building a quality discussion out of those guest appearances.

Google+ Hangout			
1	Video Type:		
2	Chat Topic:		
3	Guest List:		
4	Date:		
5	Time:		
6	Budget:		
7	Hashtag:		
8	Scripting:		

Often Google+ Hangouts go better if you prepare a list of questions for your guests to answer before they appear on your "show." Script the questions, and ask for responses to check what will be said. Then confirm the dates and times with your guests.

- Reach out to bloggers and experts on Google for this by using the email outreach template you have created. Just modify the message to suit your needs.

Hangout Questions:	Guest Responses:
1	
2	
3	
4	
5	
6	
7	
8	
9	
10	

A Pinterest Story Exercise

DAY 61

Enhance your event promotion using Pinterest as a key platform for viral sharing. These exercises will help you plan and execute quality events on Pinterest.

1 day

Create a successful blog tour image for Pinterest promotion by selecting a format:

Use Pinterest to promote an event around your book.

- Create your images in Photoshop.
- Make sure that they can be scaled down and still have impact.
- A new event means a new image.
- A single blog tour can have 50 promotional images.
- A short blog tour can begin with three images.

Blog Tour Image Creation Options		Checklist
1	Image showing you on a blog tour with guest stops	
2	Twitter chat image with incentive	
3	Google+ Hangouts image with incentive	
4	Guest blog appearance with incentive	
5	LinkedIn group discussion image	
6	Facebook chat or group image with incentive	
7	Live event: series of 10 photographs snapped on location	
8	Guest appearance on a podcast image	
9	Guest appearance in a YouTube video image	
10	Incentive images for events	

Facebook Event Preparation

Create hype for a real world event by inviting people on Facebook and using the timeline there to generate interest and virality.

 1 day

 *Set up a Facebook event.*

Facebook Event Details Date:		
1	Event Name:	
2	Event Date:	
3	Event Time:	
4	Event Guests:	
5	Event Invite Count:	
6	Confirmed Attending:	
7	Event Location:	
8	Event Description:	
9	Event Hashtag:	
10	Event Content:	
11	Event Giveaway:	*Recommended competition incentive

In order to convert those "maybe" and "decline" invites into "attending," you will need to create media to post on your Facebook event page. Here is your Facebook event content pack.

Facebook Event Media		Checklist
1	5 x unique images based on the event	
2	1 x image of the author	
3	1 x image of all guests	
4	3 x questions around event topics	
5	3 x quotes about event topics	
6	Description of the event	
7	Description of the incentive	
8	Event cover image	
9	Video to be shared on event	
10	Sample chapter of your book	

Foursquare Strategy Training

DAY 63

You need to create a Foursquare account and then use it to attract people to your event at a specific location.

1 day

Sign up for Foursquare, and add your event.

Foursquare Page		Checklist
	Account Name:	
	Password:	
1	6 x event images	
2	1 x author photo	
3	Event description	
4	Event endorsements	
5	Event testimonials	

Create deals and rewards for attendees when they login with Foursquare, who will use it to claim your incentives. Add your incentives and deals to this list below:

Foursquare Event Incentives		Checklist
1	3 friends to retweet book image for 20% discount	
2		
3		
4		
5		
6		
7		
8		
9		
10		

Events Strategy Exercise

Now that you have your sales infrastructure in place, you need a basic events strategy so that you can make sure you will have people showing up at your event. Here is how.

 3 days

 *Promote an offline event online using your new sales infrastructure!*

Event Media Pack		Platform	Checklist
1	5 x blog posts around event topics	Blog	
2	2 x email event promotions	Email	
3	2 x talking head videos promoting the event	YouTube	
4	1 x 30-second event advertisement	YouTube	
5	10 x Facebook posts around event topic	Facebook	
6	1 x Facebook event	Facebook	
7	50 x tweets around the event (5 Vines)	Twitter	
8	1 x Twitter chat on the event	Twitter	
9	50 x Pinterest images on the event	Pinterest	
10	5 x Pinterest promotional images	Pinterest	
11	5 x group chats on the event	LinkedIn	
12	5 x blog reposts on the event	LinkedIn	
13	10 x Google+ posts around the event topics	Google+	
14	1 x Google Hangout with experts	Google+	
15	1 x event incentive/reward campaign	Foursquare	
16	1 x podcast on event	Blog	

THE
ADVERTISING
BLUEPRINT

"The secret of all effective originality in advertising is not the creation of new and tricky words and pictures, but one of putting familiar words and pictures into new relationships."
LEO BURNETT

Writing a book is a triumph, but advertising it until it becomes popular is just as much of an art form. Having a good book product is key, although you will need a lot of advertising orientation to get the results that you deserve.

In order to correctly advertise your book product, you need modeling tools to plan and execute an effective advertising strategy. This part of the workbook helps you do just that while orientating you on how much money you should be investing in direct advertising.

Financial Investment Determination

You need to determine how much money you want to spend on paid advertising. Like it or not, paid ads will get you results. They are a critical part of your short-term sales strategy for your book online.

Test your paid advertising skills, and analyze your results afterwards to adjust your budget. Here you need to take your $1000 (or other allotted amount) and split it according to your chosen ad platforms.

1 day

Take $1000, and see what you can do with it.

Ad Platform Total Budget:		Budget	Checklist
1	Google AdSense		
2	Media Net		
3	Chitika		
4	Infolinks		
5	Clicksor		
6	Facebook ads		
7	YouTube ads		
8	Twitter ads		
9	LinkedIn ads		
10	Direct blog advertising		

Now calculate the return on investment from each of these networks:

Ad Platform		ROI Results
1	Google AdSense	
2	Media Net	
3	Chitika	
4	Infolinks	
5	Clicksor	
6	Facebook ads	
7	YouTube ads	
8	Twitter ads	
9	LinkedIn ads	
10	Direct blog advertising	

The Google AdWords Exercise

On a tight budget, Pay Per Click ads are the best form of advertising around. Here is how to create your first PPC ad.

 1 day

- Begin by learning all you can about Google AdWords.
- Create two ads or more at a time to split test them concurrently to see what works best.

Create your book PPC ad.

Then identify your target keywords and create your text ad below:

Google AdWords Ad Creation			
1	Keyword: *Choose one main keyword*		
2	Headline: *25 characters*		
3	Body Text: *Line one, 35 characters*		
4	Body Text: *Line two, 35 characters*		
5	Device:		
6	Landing Page URL:		

*Remember, the goal of this advertisement is to get clicks, not to sell your book!

YouTube Advertising Training

The trick with TrueView YouTube ads is to target them correctly, which means that keywords and audience targeting are crucial to your success.

1 day

TrueView ads come in a range of formats, but they are essentially "cost-per-view" ads that play on a YouTube video. You can bid for the show price and keyword relevance. These ads can also appear on video publisher pages as part of the Google Display Network.

To create a functional YouTube TrueView ad

This type of ad is for video promotion—use it to get more views of your videos!

To stay on budget, keep your ads under 30 seconds long to avoid having to pay when people do not watch your entire ad.

	TrueView Instream Ad Guidelines	Checklist
1	Bid on the best possible keyword.	
2	State your entire ad message in a 5-second intro.	
3	Add a call to action button in your video advert.	
4	Keep your ad under 30 seconds long.	
5	Set your maximum cost per view.	
6	Set the right gender.	
7	Set the right age group.	
8	Set the right parental status.	
9	Set the most appropriate interests.	
10	Set the most specific topics.	
11	Use remarketing to get people to come back.	
12	Target content related to your chosen keywords.	
13	Target specific videos and websites.	

Naturally, you need to think about your target audience and determine the following:

Your Video Target Audience: Answer These Questions	
1	What is the dominant gender of your buyer?	
2	How old is the most important age group?	
3	What is the parental status of your core buyer?	
4	What are your buyer's main interests in life?	
5	What topics are relevant to yours?	
6	What keywords are related to your book?	
7	Which videos and websites would your buying public be on?	

Facebook Ad Training

It is time to create your first Facebook ad that leads back to your book landing page. Again, targeting is important, so use the information you uncovered for your text and YouTube videos to inform your targeting decisions here.

Invest $150 in a Facebook ad, and create two of them.

 1 day

 To create your first Facebook ad

Facebook Ad Creation		Your Research Here
1	Choose your objective:	
2	Name your campaign:	
3	Your audience location:	
4	Your audience age:	
5	Your audience gender:	
6	Your audience interests:	
7	Your audience connections:	
8	Your audience language:	
9	Your audience behavior:	
10	Your audience categories:	
11	Set your daily budget:	
12	Choose an ad image:	
13	Write the content for your ad:	• Create a clear action. • Highlight benefits. • Use a striking image. • Include your book title.

Advertising Strategy Exercise

By focusing on your analytics, you will see where paid advertising can step in and plug your content holes. If you need more fans on Facebook, for example, you can get them quickly simply by opting for paid advertising for a month or two.

 *1 day*

This ad strategy is meant to be used when you have an event coming up or when you have discovered a fault in your sales funnel. For example, if you are getting a lot of leads from everywhere but Pinterest, but the leads you get from Pinterest tend to buy more often, you can use paid advertising to boost your followers there and, eventually, your sales.

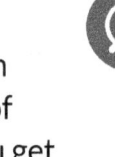 *Have an ad strategy at the ready.*

Step-by-Step Ad Strategy Checklist	Checklist
1 Locate the error in your sales funnel.	
2 Find better keywords to use.	
3 Research that specific market segment.	
4 Identify your platform audience.	
5 Create your platform buyer persona.	
6 Select your ad format.	
7 Set a budget.	
8 Select the appropriate targets.	
9 Create 2–4 ads, and run them concurrently.	
10 Measure the results.	
11 Pick the best ad, and run it for longer.	
12 Get more sales.	

Split Testing Exercise

Split testing helps you optimize your advertisements and other content so that it performs better for you online. You will need two ads to see how this works.

For this split test, you will create two Google AdWords ads and run them at the same time, splitting your traffic between the two. As the three days pass, you will see which ad is best.

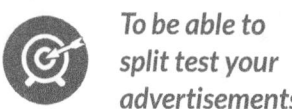

3 days

To be able to split test your advertisements

The Split Test Google AdWords Ad Creation			
1	Keyword: *Choose one main keyword*		
2	Headline: *25 characters*		
3	Body Text: *Line one, 35 characters*		
4	Body Text: *Line two, 35 characters*		
5	Device:		
6	Landing Page URL:		

THE
EXPOSURE
BLUEPRINT

"But I work harder now because I have so much more exposure. And actually the harder you work as a writer, the better you get at it. It's like anything else. It's a muscle you have to exercise. I write more now than ever."

RON WHITE

In order to reach that elusive pinnacle as an author and to achieve bestselling status, you need to pursue the height of exposure with all of your marketing might until it happens. Exposure means putting yourself and your book out there for the world to see.

In this part of your workbook, you will learn some important functional tools that will help you gain and retain exposure among specific communities of people. These people will become your long-term reading public, and they will spread your name and works far and wide.

Article Marketing Blueprint

Do not post duplicate articles on article marketing websites. Instead, create unique posts, and spread them throughout your article websites evenly. Fifteen articles a week should be great, and you can divide them between your sites.

Come up with 15 unique titles based around your book. You can segment them into different topics if you like; it is up to you. Write them here along with your chosen link (where the article will point to, such as your book landing page) and your keywords.

 1 day

 *To boost your book website's SEO and to create lead generation*

Article Marketing Topics	Links	Keywords
1		
2		
3		
4		
5		
6		
7		
8		
9		
10		
11		
12		
13		
14		
15		

Article Distribution Plan Exercise

DAY
76

Do not post duplicate articles on article marketing websites. Instead, create unique posts, and spread them throughout your article websites evenly. Fifteen articles a week should be great, and you can divide them between your sites.

1 day

Come up with 15 unique titles based around your book. You can segment them into different topics if you like; it is up to you. Write them here along with your chosen link (where the article will point to, such as your book landing page) and your keywords.

To create 10 different article topic groups

Article Topic Groups	
1	
2	
3	
4	
5	
6	
7	
8	
9	
10	

Now take one topic group and create 10 titles for it to see how it works.

Article Marketing Topics Group 1: [TOPIC]	Links	Keywords
1		
2		
3		
4		
5		
6		
7		
8		
9		
10		

Each group belongs on a specific article platform. Choose from these:

Article Marketing Platforms		
1	EzineArticles.com	
2	Hubpages.com	
3	Squidoo.com	
4	ArticleBase.com	
5	Ehow.com	
6	Buzzle.com	
7	Examiner.com	
8	Helium.com	
9	Goarticles.com	

The Slideshare Strategy

Sign up and record your Slideshare.net details. Then create your first 10-slide "slidedeck" using this strategy. This can be used on your blog, on Slideshare, and on your social media pages.

You must have Microsoft PowerPoint to create your slides.

 1 day

 Sign up to Slideshare.net, and create a slideshow strategy.

Slideshare Account		Checklist
	Account Name:	
	Password:	
1	6 x book images	
2	1 x author profile photo	
3	Book blurb	
4	Book endorsements	
5	Book testimonials	
6	Social media links	
7	Website link and contact details	

Now create your first slideshow strategy by filling in the following:

Slideshow Strategy		
1	Slideshow Title:	
2	Number of Slides:	
3	Slideshow category:	
4	Target audience:	
5	Marketing goal:	
6	Slideshow images:	
7	Slideshow links:	
8	Slideshow video:	
9	Slideshow keywords:	
10	Full slideshow text:	

Google Alerts Exercise

Create your Google Alerts keyword list, and be notified on important news, changes, and opportunities in your niche. Being informed is half the battle!

1 day

Build your Google Alert Keyword List

Your First 5 Google Keyword Alerts	Date Set
1	
2	
3	
4	
5	

Flickr and Instagram Strategy

DAY 79

Sign up to Flickr or Instagram, and set up your account. Then funnel your real-world images through Instagram or Flickr, and use them in your media.

1 day

Sign up and set up your Instagram and Flickr Accounts.

Instagram Account		Checklist
	Account Name:	
	Password:	
1	6 x book images	
2	1 x author photo	
3	Book blurb/one-line description	
4	Website link	
5	Follow 300 relevant people.	
6	Take 20 fresh photos for your account.	

Flickr Account		Checklist
	Account Name:	
	Password:	
1	6 x book images	
2	1 x author photo	
3	Book blurb and description	
4	Book endorsements	
5	Book testimonials	
6	Upload all relevant book and marketing photos.	

The Top 40 Websites List

 DAY **80** - DAY **81**

 *2 days*

Keep all of your important login details in a safe place for your marketing campaigns. Sign up to these 40 websites, and record your login details.

Sign up and create accounts on these platforms.

	Book Website Login Details	Account Name:	Password:
1	BookTalk.org		
2	Goodreads.com		
3	Kindleboards		
4	WritersNet		
5	LibraryThing		
6	Booksie		
7	Nothing Binding		
8	Authonomy		
9	Bibliophil		
10	Wattpad		
11	BookBrowse		
12	Scribd		
13	Filed by		
14	Book Buzzr		
15	Figment		
16	Tim Greaton Forum		
17	Bookreportradio		
18	WhoWroteWhat		
19	SavvyBookwriters Blog		
20	Jacket Flap		
21	Bookhitch		

22	Absolutewrite.com Forums		
23	Freebooksy		
24	Bookandreader.com		
25	Blog.booksontheknob.org		
26	Authormarketingclub.com		
27	Writing.com		
28	Reading-forum.co.uk		
29	Addictedtoebooks.com		
30	Canadianbookclubs.com		
31	Online-literature.com Forums		
32	Thebookmarketingnetwork.com Forums		
33	Bookforum.com		
34	Thefrugalreader.wufoo.com		
35	Kindlemojo.com		
36	Flurriesofwords.blogspot.ca		
37	Thekindledailydeal.com		
38	Ebookforum.info		
39	Bookgrouponline.com		
40	Bookclubforum.co.uk		

Book Club Sites Compilation

Here you will choose which book clubs to approach to request that they consider your book for their book club this month, at a discount for bulk sales of course.

1 day

To reach out to book clubs and convert them into buyers

Book Club List Selection	
1	Wearetbc.com
2	Shelfari.com
3	GoodReads Groups
4	Scholastic Book Clubs
5	Richard and Judy
6	Double Day Book Club
7	The BBC 4 Bookclub
8	The Literary Guild Book Club
9	The Big Book Club
10	*Facebook-based book clubs

Now create you outreach email, and offer them a friendly incentive.

Hi [NAME],

This is who you are and why you are reaching out to them.
Add in your credentials, and be passionate about your book.

Add in any prominent endorsements or testimonials from known experts.
Ask them if they would consider adding your book to their book club list.
Then offer them a discount or an incentive.

Attach a sample chapter for them to review.
Mention that it is also in audio if they need it.

A warm sign off.

CHAPTER 12

THE INCENTIVES BLUEPRINT

"If you look at history, innovation doesn't come just from giving people incentives; it comes from creating environments where their ideas can connect."

STEVEN JOHNSON

Incentives prompt action, and in strong marketing campaigns, they can make even the most doubtful buyer invest in the product. There is no doubt that understanding how to use marketing incentives with your book will increase your sales.

When your book provides so much value, it seems as though the reader is getting a huge deal—this is when you sell the most books. This part of the workbook will help you plan and execute some critical steps in the incentives creation and integration process.

Incentives Determination

Create content incentives to help your marketing efforts succeed. These will encourage readers to click, sign up, subscribe, and buy more often.

I strongly recommend getting quotes to have these created for you.

 1 day

 *Choose which incentives to use in your marketing efforts*

Incentives Content Pack	
10 Pieces of Incentive Content	**Cost**
1 1 x 5-page mini ebook on a relevant subject	
2 1 x audio podcast (tips, interviews, discussions)	
3 1 x audio podcast (tips, interviews, discussions)	
4 1 x audio podcast (tips, interviews, discussions)	
5 1 x 20-page ebook on a relevant subject	
6 1 x 20-page ebook on a relevant subject	
7 1 x long-form showcase post on industry expert	
8 1 x long-form showcase post on industry expert	
9 1 x long-form showcase post on industry expert	
10 1 x viral video ad for YouTube	

All of these incentives will drive traffic to Amazon if you use them as instructed. Keep in mind that these need to be high quality because they will eventually be the media that convinces a person to buy your book.

Facebook Incentives Exercise

DAY
84

Your Facebook fan page need to contain a large number of fans if your marketing is going to be successful there. I want you to consider aiming for a community of at least 1,000–2,000 people within these initial 90 days. Do not buy your fans; they will not buy from you.

 1 day

 To get fans on your Facebook page

Create a Facebook competition to stimulate fan subscriber rates:

Facebook Competition Creation	
1	Competition goal:
2	Competition reward:
3	Competition length:
4	Competition colors:
5	Competition image:
6	Competition video:
7	Competition slogan:
8	Competition entry details:
9	Competition terms:
10	Competition text: (aim for 100 words)

Twitter Incentives Exercise

Create one of these incentives for your Twitter page, and enjoy the boost in follows that you get. Make sure that the person that gets your incentive tweets about it.

 1 day

Budget for these Twitter incentives.

 *To get followers on your Twitter page*

Twitter Incentive Creation		Cost
1	A powerful call to action tweet followed by a bit.ly link and a 30% discount offer	
2	10% coupon on your website/sales page. A positive tweet about the book gets readers a coupon for a discount.	
3	Retweet events photos at a book signing to gain a chance to win a prize.	
4	Very active Twitter uses will be offered free giveaways in return for positive tweets.	
5	Include direct download links to your incentive content for quick Twitter downloads for fans. These tweets will be shared.	
6	Get email sign-ups when you offer Twitter followers a discount to retweet your landing page.	

Website Incentives Exercise

DAY
86

Select an incentive strategy for your website and blog, and use it to improve the conversions on your key pages. Get more clicks, sign-ups, and sales.

1 day

Establish your website-based incentive strategy

Website Incentives Pack		
1	Incentives budget:	
2	Pages that need boosting:	
3	Content creator:	
Incentive Content Selection		**Cost**
1	1 x 5-page mini ebook	
2	1 x 10-page mini ebook	
3	1 x 20-page mini ebook	
4	1 x sample chapter for your book	
5	1 x competition with a prize	
6	1 x mini course on related subject	
7	1 x industry whitepaper	
8	1 x podcast series	
9	1 x video clip series	
10	1 x free audio book chapter	

Once you have decided on your incentives, you will need to figure out where best to use them on your website. There are many locations that would do the trick.

Areas where you can use these incentives:

1	Email sign-up form	6	In your newsletter prompt
2	Opt-in form	7	Dedicated landing page
3	Beneath a blog post	8	In your footer
4	In a hosted advertisement	9	In your header
5	On your homepage slider	10	In your website sidebar

Event Incentives Exercise

DAY 87

Take your marketing on the road when you start using incentives at events. Author marketers are not used to promoting themselves or their products, so it can be a rocky road. But you get a lot more conversions in person than you can get online.

1 day

To select event incentives for your next appearance

Remember, people always recall how you made them feel. Incentives make them feel special, so it pays to come bearing gifts.

Remember, people always recall how you made them feel. Incentives make them feel special, so it pays to come bearing gifts.

Places Where Incentives Encourage Sales		
1	Live general events	
2	Conferences	
3	A book signing	
4	A special appearance	
5	A workshop	
6	A seminar	
7	A networking event	
8	A retail appearance	
9	A blog tour stop	
10	A meetup	

Each month, set a small amount of money aside for prizes, and jot down if you experience any boom in sales because of these live event giveaways. Interestingly enough, a lot of media can be generated from live giveaways, which has a positive spin-off impact on social media. This is great for sales!

Budgeting for Competitions

Monthly Competition Budget	ROI
1	
2	
3	
4	
5	
6	
7	
8	
9	
10	

Keep track of who you give free copies of your book to, and ask them for photos of themselves with the book.

Free Book Incentive	Photo URL
1	
2	
3	
4	
5	
6	
7	
8	
9	
10	

The Top 40 Websites List

You have reached the last four days of your epic marketing campaign! Use this excellent checklist to make sure that all of your strategies are on the go and working for your bottom line.

 *3 days*

 Monitor and maintain your marketing campaign

- Remember to check on your SEO every three months.
- Reinvest some of the profits from your book into expanding your sales funnel or improving it.
- There is nothing "automatic" about book sales. You have to work on them!
- On the last day of every month, make a point of reviewing all of your online platforms.

Marketing Strategies On the Go		Checklist
1	Learn new selling techniques, and improve existing selling techniques.	
2	Check on your SEO strategy at least four times a year. There are always keyword changes.	
3	Check on your Amazon, eBay, Clickbank, Lulu, and other accounts. Are sales increasing or dead?	
4	Check on your iTunes and audio sales. If these can be improved, then invest more in them.	
5	Focus on your social media accounts daily. Create great content, and share it.	
6	Focus on your blog daily, and create excellent quality posts for your readership.	

Marketing Strategies On the Go		Checklist
7	Check on your website and blog traffic. Split test and improve conversions there every month.	
8	Check on your advertising performance each week. Split test and improve conversions there too.	
9	Split test your sales and landing pages to get your conversions rate high.	
10	After your 90-day campaign, schedule your blog tour. Make appearances where you can, when you can.	
11	Focus on getting on traditional media spots. Television, the news, and radio are all important.	

CONCLUSION

Excellent! Your hard work is going to pay off any day now.

This workbook has provided you with the essential tools that you need to record critical information, to conduct important research, and to plan for the implementation of specific marketing techniques.

Working concurrently with your 90-Day Plan to Marketing Your Book, you have an all-in-one system for learning how to promote and sell more copies of your book. I want you to keep this workbook close by because the information inside it will change.

I highly suggest printing it out, writing directly in the allotted spaces, and keeping these as your personal record of your campaign strategy. As your marketing infrastructure evolves and your sales grow, you will want to refer back to this document to see where it all began.

Keep in mind that you may have enormous success with one specific branch of marketing, in which case it makes sense for you to divert your budget, time, and resources to that specific technique because it works for you.

It also helps if you are able to eventually hire a person to manage your blog and social media so that you have more time to dedicate to marketing. Content creation is important, but it does become a roadblock to effective marketing because it is time consuming.

That is why I suggest you put aside some of your book sales earnings and begin to hire a reliable freelancer to create your incentives, posts, and social updates for you based on the plan that you have outlined in this book.

By delegating these lesser tasks, you can free up your time and spend it wisely by focusing on analytics and conversion optimization. If you can get a 30% conversion rate (like many of the pro marketers do) on your sales page, for example, you will make a fortune from your many traffic streams that you have painstakingly put together here.

Your book has every chance of becoming a bestseller. The only thing that remains is for you to take this information, this strategy, and this content—and to go and get those sales!

To your success!

-Melissa Se

REFERENCES

Education, BrainyQuote, http://www.brainyquote.com/quotes/topics/topic_education.html

Marketing, BrainyQuote, http://www.brainyquote.com/quotes/keywords/marketing.html

Marketing, BrainyQuote, http://www.brainyquote.com/quotes/keywords/marketing.html

Quotebank: Digital, http://www.warc.com/Pages/NewsAndOpinion/Quotebank.aspx?Category=Digital

Scheidies, Nick, *Top 40 Blogging Quotes*, http://www.incomediary.com/bloggerstop-blogging-quotes

Libert, Kelsey, *The Blogger Outreach Equation*, https://moz.com/blog/the-blogger-outreach-equation

Free Meta Tag Tool, http://tools.seobook.com/meta-medic/

YouTube, BrainyQuote, http://www.brainyquote.com/quotes/keywords/youtube.html

Events, BrainyQuote, http://www.brainyquote.com/quotes/keywords/cvcnts.html

Advertising, BrainyQuote, http://www.brainyquote.com/quotes/keywords/advertising.html

Exposure, BrainyQuote, http://www.brainyquote.com/quotes/keywords/exposure.html

Incentives, BrainyQuote, http://www.brainyquote.com/quotes/keywords/incentives.html

ABOUT THE AUTHOR

Melissa Se, is a Vancouver-based award-winning writer who enjoys the challenges of creativity and attention to detail. She dedicates her time to helping people publish & market their books effectively. In her spare time, she can be found dining out with her husband, walking her delightful dogs, or voraciously reading anywhere comfy. If you have a story to tell and want to get published, Melissa and her team can help you ghostwrite, edit, design, and publish your book in 90 days. *She can be reached at melissa@the-best-sellers.com*